William Clint

The Aborigines of Canada Under the British Crown

with a glance at their customs, characteristics, and history

William Clint

The Aborigines of Canada Under the British Crown
with a glance at their customs, characteristics, and history

ISBN/EAN: 9783337273064

Printed in Europe, USA, Canada, Australia, Japan

Cover: Foto ©Andreas Hilbeck / pixelio.de

More available books at **www.hansebooks.com**

THE
ABORIGINES OF CANADA

UNDER THE BRITISH CROWN,

WITH A GLANCE AT THEIR CUSTOMS, CHARACTERISTICS, AND HISTORY;

BY

WILLIAM CLINT,

(READ BEFORE THE SOCIETY, 23RD MARCH, 1878.)

THE question of our relations with the Indian inhabitants of this vast country should be an interesting one. It should be interesting firstly because on us, as Christians, the duty seems to have been imposed of leading these people out of the darkness of heathenism and superstition to a knowledge of the Christian religion, of raising them from their squalor and ignorance to an improved position physically, socially and mentally, and of preparing them for the exercise of those rights of citizenship which are the birthright of intelligent British subjects of every color and creed. The subject should be especially interesting too, because it has fallen to the lot of the present generation to open out for settlement the great North-West, the future garden of the Dominion, and we are thus brought face to face with the Indian in his native wilds. It is necessary that the Indian hunting-ground should be in a large measure given up to the plough and sickle of the White man ; it has been so ordered by Providence, doubtless for the ultimate good of the Indian himself, as well as the White man ; but it is not necessary that this result should be accomplished by a system of spoliation and extermination. On the contrary, animated as we should be by that spirit of justice and fair-play which so strongly characterizes that great nation of which we are proud to form a part—that generous spirit which secures the weak from oppression on the part of the strong—we should see that if we are obliged to encroach upon territory hitherto occupied by the Red man, we give him a fair equivalent for what we get; that if we deprive him of his accustomed means of subsistence we place within his reach other means, which will finally obtain for him more comfort, more independence, and more happiness, and that we treat him in all respects as men should do who are themselves free-born citizens of an enlightened, freedom-loving, Christian state. The Indians should in fact be made to feel that under the folds of the Union Jack they are the equals of any in the land, so long as they obey laws framed with the object of protecting the Red man from injustice on the part of the White just as fully and firmly as they would afford protection to the White man if threatened by the Red. The eyes of other nations are upon us, and according to our action in these respects will they judge us; nay, according to our action in this matter will we judge ourselves, nationally and individually, and according to it too will we be judged by posterity.

We have, I think, no reason to feel ashamed of the course of the representatives of British authority towards the aboriginal tribes. Throughout this broad country we have at present no portion of them in arms against us, or at enmity with us; on the contrary, we have permanently attracted, so far as can be seen at present, their respect and good-will. How then has this result been arrived at?

I propose in this paper to consider as briefly as possible the original inhabitants of this country, their distinguishing characteristics and customs, and the relations with the

European of those who occupied the older provinces during the eventful period of the French *régime*, to discover the whereabouts of the remnants of these once powerful tribes, their present condition, and what has been done for them by our Government, and finally to consider the dealings of the authorities with the Indian tribes of the great North-West.

The term "Indian" originally came to be applied to the aborigines of this continent by Columbus and the early discoverers, because they imagined that the newly-found countries were parts of Asia or the "Indies," and though this was soon afterwards found to be an error, the term had become established, and has since continued in use. The Indians formed a peculiar variety of the human species, differing, though not very widely, from the Mongolian. It has been ascertained upon investigation of the different dialects in use in North America that there were eight aboriginal mother tongues, and this fact would seem to indicate that there were the same number of distinct branches or families. The new world is believed to have been peopled from the old, and considering that the Mongol race was situated nearest the point where Asia and America approach very closely to each other, and the points of resemblance between the two races, it is natural to suppose that the Indians were of Mongolian extraction, and had originally found their way across the narrow channel which divides the two continents. The points of difference between the two races are easily accounted for by reason of the change of outward circumstances, and although the variety of dialect amongst the Indian tribes would seem to militate against the idea of common extraction and the one route of immigration, yet on the other hand the theory is supported by the strong resemblance there was in the appearance, habits, and ideas, of all the Indian tribes from the St. Lawrence to the Gulf of Mexico.

The face was broad and flat, with high cheek-bones, more rounded and arched than in the allied type, without having the visage expanded to the same breadth. The forehead was generally low and narrow, the eyes deep, small, and of dark or light hazel color, the nose rather diminutive, but prominent, with wide nostrils, the mouth large, and lips thick, the expression stern and fierce. The stature, though variable in different parts of the continent, was in the country we now inhabit generally above the middle size in the men, though the women were usually below that standard, a fact which may probably be ascribed to the drudgery they were obliged to undergo. The colour of the skin was red or copper-coloured, a tint which was not altogether ascribable to the influence of sun, rain, and wind, but is said to have been to a great extent artificially produced by dissolving the juice of a root with the oil, grease, &c., with which they were accustomed to besmear their persons. The hair, like that of the allied type, the Mongols, was coarse, black, thin, but long. Like the latter also, by a curious coincidence, most of them removed it from every part of the head with the exception of a tuft on the crown, which they cherished with much care. Any possibility of beard was carefully obviated by pulling out the hairs from the face as fast as they appeared; this probably that there should be no obstacle to the painting of the face according to custom. They were capable of long-continued exertion, an individual having been known to travel nearly eighty miles in a day without symptom of fatigue; and they were also capable of extraordinary abstinence from food. Their covering was chiefly the skins of wild animals, whilst their bodies were painted in fantastic fashion, and generally had a representation of the guardian spirit of the individual, the animal that formed the symbol of their tribe, and the enemies whom the warrior may have slain and scalped in battle. They subsisted by means of the chase, some tribes only devoting themselves slightly to agriculture, which consisted chiefly in growing *maize*, and the labour of which devolved almost entirely on the women. In their native state they were not acquainted with any species of intoxicating liquor. Their dwellings were cabins or huts made from the bark of trees. Of domestic animals they had the dog, which they made useful in hunting, and occasionally made a meal of; the horse was unknown until after the arrival of Europeans in the country.

Their government was democratic in the extreme, in spirit though not in form, each individual being free to do as he pleased, even to the wounding or murder of a neighbour with whom he may have had a controversy, though in this case the injury would be speedily avenged by the kindred of the injured person, the episode scarcely ruffling the general tranquillity, or else the life taken was atoned for by presents of a fixed value made up from among the tribe, and especially was this done if the murdered man had belonged to another tribe. Sometimes however such outrages brought on wars between different tribes. But, notwithstanding this individual freedom, the strictest order existed in their communities, the absence of any restraint of law being made up for by a strong feeling of clannish attachment, binding the members of one tribe to each other, and also by that sense of dignity and self-command which they considered inseparable from the character of a warrior. As Parkman says, in speaking of the Iroquois : " An " explanation of this harmony is to be found also in an in- " tense spirit of nationality, for never since the days of " Sparta were individual life and national life more com- " pletely fused into one."

They were generous in relieving each other's necessities, and in caring for the children of relatives or members of the same tribe killed in battle. Polygamy was almost unknown among the tribes in the vicinity of the Lakes. They were tender in their domestic relations, although all outward exhibition of this tenderness was studiously suppressed, as unbecoming the character of warriors. The exertion however of the father for the welfare of his family, and eagerness to avenge their wrongs, sufficiently proved that this apathy was far more apparent than real.

The mental faculties of the Indians were developed in a comparatively remarkable degree. The manner in which they would follow out a direct line through the pathless forest, the geographical knowledge they attained in their wanderings, the political acumen they displayed in their measures for the aggrandizement of their own tribe and the humbling of their enemies, their oratorical powers in the use of their unwritten, and limited, but figurative language, were such as to command the admiration and surprise of Europeans.

They believed in the existence of a Great Spirit, or Supreme Ruler of the Universe, though their application of the term rendered in our language " Spirit" did not necessarily convey the idea of an immaterial nature. The lamented Thomas D'Arcy McGee, in some pretty stanzas, entitled: " The Arctic Indian's Faith," outlines the Indian's ideas on this head.

> " We worship the Spirit that walks unseen
> Through our land of ice and snow;
> We know not His face, we know not His place,
> But His presence and power we know.
>
> Does the Buffalo need the Pale-face Word
> To find his pathway far?
> What guide has he to the hidden ford,
> Or where the green pastures are?
> Who teacheth the Moose that the hunter's gun
> Is peering out of the shade?
> Who teacheth the doe and the fawn to run
> In the track the Moose has made?
>
> Him do we follow, Him do we fear,
> The Spirit of earth and sky;
> Who hears with the Wapiti's eager ear

His poor red children's cry ;
Whose whisper we note in every breeze
That stirs the birch canoe ;
Who hangs the rein-deer moss on the trees
For the food of the *Caribou.*

That Spirit we worship who walks unseen
Through our land of ice and snow ;
We know not His face, we know not His place,
But His presence and power we know."

But though the Indian had some idea of a supreme over-
ruling Spirit, his belief was involved in much mystery and
superstition.   He spiritualized all nature.   Birds and beasts,
and even inanimate objects, such as lakes, rivers, forests,
could be the home of the great Spirit, or might have a
spiritual nature, a soul of their own, to be propitiated by
prayers and offerings. The Good Spirit was looked to to give
good fortune, success in battle, and in the chase, courage
amid tortures, &c., whilst any unpropitious event was re-
garded as the result of the anger of the Good Spirit, or of
the machinations of an Evil Spirit, and the Spirit had accordingly to be appeased by offerings, it might be of a frag-
ment of meat thrown into the fire and burned that the
Spirit might partake of it, or an offering of tobacco thrown
into a river, or in some other way. The *manitou*, or guardian power, was an object of great veneration. It might
be the head or claw of a bird, or a fish, serpent, or other
object which would be impressed on the mind of a youth
in a dream after he had undergone a preparatory fast of
several days, and which would thereafter be looked upon
as his special guardian spirit, and expected to aid him in
every emergency.

They believed in a future life, a brighter land, a happy
hunting-ground, where the spirit of the warrior who had
borne himself bravely in battle, or unflinchingly undergone
torture at the hands of his enemies should at last arrive,
after having surmounted several obstacles on the way, to

find game in abundance, and perpetual freedom from hunger and cold, from sickness, and suffering, and war. The dim tradition of a creation, and of a general deluge was also handed down by the Indian from generation to generation.

They had great reverence for the dead, whom they interred in the richest robes, and with all their arms and ornaments supposed to be necessary for their use in the happy hunting-grounds, and the bones of their fathers were considered as one of the strongest ties to their native soil.

They had great faith in dreams, and before engaging in war, the chase, or any other undertaking, the dreams of the principal chiefs were carefully noted, and the conduct of the tribe shaped in accordance with their interpretation. Charlevoix relates that when Sir William Johnson during the American war was negotiating an alliance with a friendly tribe, the chief confidentially disclosed that during his slumbers he had been favoured with a vision of Sir William bestowing upon him the rich laced coat which formed his full dress. The fulfilment of this revelation was very inconvenient, yet on being assured that it positively occurred the English Commander found it advisable to resign his uniform. Soon after however, he unfolded to the Indian a dream with which he had himself been favored, and in which the former was seen presenting him with a large tract of fertile land most commodiously situated. The native ruler admitted that since the vision had been vouchsafed it must be realized, but earnestly proposed to cease this mutual dreaming which he found had turned much to his own disadvantage.

But that which presented the character of the Indian in its darkest aspect was his warfare. The deadliest enmity occasionally sprung up between tribes, caused either by individual acts of provocation, encroachments on one another's hunting grounds, the desire of extending the power of a tribe, or even a thirst for glory or excitement. The Indians rarely fought pitched battles; their warfare took the from rather of skirmishes, surprises, ambuscades, and sudden forays into each other's hunting grounds and villages. When once hostilities had begun the predominating passion was revenge. Having taken measures to learn the will of the Great Spirit, and provided the result was favorable, the war-chief who was elected by the warriors on account of his experience, military renown, commanding stature, &c., immediately entered on a course of preparation. He was painted in bright and varied colors, red predominating; he endured long fasts, and took particular note of his dreams. A huge fire was kindled, whereon was placed the great war-cauldron, into which every one present threw something. The chief sang the war-song, and the warriors joined in the war-dance, after which a solemn feast of dogs' flesh was held, during which former exploits were recounted, and those they expected to achieve dilated upon. The females occupied themselves in negotiating for a supply of captives on whom to wreak their vengeance, and appease the shades of their slain relatives, and all preliminaries being completed the leader started on the march singing his war-song, while the others followed, at intervals sounding the war-whoop. On entering hostile territory they crept along in the deepest silence, keeping close together, watching each twig and tuft of grass for any sign of the trail of an enemy which they were adepts in discovering. As the Indians seldom posted sentries, trusting entirely for safety to the protection of their guardian spirits, it was an easy matter to surprise a hostile village. Having made their way then to the vicinity of their enemy's village without previous discovery, they would secrete themselves in the forest until the small hours of the morning, and then throwing themselves upon the village like so many fiends, with arrows, tomahawks, and war-clubs, they soon despatched the majority of the inhabitants.

2

They contrived to capture as many fugitives as possible alive, in order that they might be subjected on the return home of the war-party to all the refinements of cruel torture that diabolical minds could conceive, tortures in which the women took a chief part, to revenge themselves for the loss of their husbands and brothers in the battle. These tortures were borne with the most heroic courage, the unfortunate captive singing his death-song, recounting his warlike exploits, and the cruelties his people had inflicted on the friends of his tormentors, and daring the latter to do their worst. At times it happened that a captive instead of being tortured, was adopted into one of the families of his captors, to replace one who had perished in the engagement, and in such case he became thereafter a regular member of the tribe. The Iroquois particularly were in the habit of adopting prisoners at times, as they thus were enabled to offset their large losses in their numerous wars. Sometimes portions of the flesh of prisoners were eaten, but it does not appear that cannibalism as a practice can be charged against the Indians.

When necessary for the accomplishment of their ends, they did not hesitate to use treachery; on the other hand many instances are on record illustrative of the sway of the principle of honor among them. An example or two may not be out of place. In 1663 a party of Iroquois was on the way to negotiate a peace with the French, when some Algonquins, stung by their wrongs, formed an ambuscade, and violated the character of the mission by killing the majority of the party. In 1645 two war parties—Huron and Iroquois—met in the forest: the Hurons fought so well as nearly to have gained the day, when the Iroquois called for a parley to treat for peace, and when the chiefs of the opposite party had sat down to a council they fell on them, and killed or captured a considerable number. On the other hand Parkman relates that an old Iroquois chief.

having been despatched as an ambassador to negotiate a treaty with the Hurons, and having a suspicion that some of the Iroquois were about to attack the Hurons, which they actually did, so felt the stain upon his honor that he committed suicide, and was found with his throat gashed from ear to ear, a victim of mortified pride. On another occasion a French Priest, who had been residing with one of the Iroquois nations, and against whom, owing to some action of the French Indians, a feeling had been raised, was, by order of the chiefs, conducted out of the country to a place of safety before this feeling could take form, in accordance with a pledge for his safety previously given. The intercourse between the Iroquois and the British Colonists also affords numerous instances of the scrupulous integrity with which the former adhered to the provisions of their treaties, or *chains*, as they called them, with the latter, a scrupulousness which might put to shame at times the dealings of the White man with his fellows.

At the time of the first settlement of Europeans on this continent, it is computed that the native inhabitants of North America did not exceed 200,000 souls. The territory then styled New France, together with the chief portion of what is now the State of New York, was chiefly divided between three great nations, the Algonquins, the Hurons, and the Iroquois or Five Nations. These were the most important, but there were also other subordinate tribes. In regard to their names and hunting grounds, the following summary is taken from Dr. Miles' History of Canada :

" In that part of New France now called Novā Scotia, in " Gaspé, and south of the St. Lawrence, the Indians were " offshoots of the great Algonquin stock, including those " named *Micmacs* or *Souriquois*, *Etchemins*, *Abenaquis*, and " *Sokokis*, to the number of about four thousand in all. " Further inland, and occupying chiefly the north bank of the

" St. Lawrence were the *Montagnais* of Saguenay and Lake
" St. John, having for neighbours to the north the *Esqui-*
" *maux* of Labrador and the regions bordering on Hudson's
" Bay. In the valley of the river St. Maurice, and occupy-
" ing the north bank of the St. Lawrence, in the vicinity of
" the site of Three Rivers, were the *Bull-heads* or *Attikame-*
" *gues.* Next to these, extending westwards along the St.
" Lawrence, and on the banks of the Ottawa were the *Al-*
" *gonquins* proper, including a tribe named *Nipissings*
" around the lake of that name. . The *Ottawas* and *Chippe-*
" *was* were near the outlet of Lake Superior, to the south of
" which lay the *Foxes*, the *Sacs*, the *Menomonees*, the *Mas-*
" *coutens* and *Kikapoos.* The *Hurons*--a term originally
" used by the French as a nickname—whose proper name
" was *Wendats*, or *Wyandots*, numbering it is believed not
" less than 30,000, occupied settlements in the peninsula
" adjacent to Lake Simcoe and Georgian Bay, having for
" neighbors on the south-west the *Tionontates* or *Petuns.*
" Next to these latter, to the south, and extending eastward
" as far as or beyond the Falls of Niagara, were a great many
" kindred tribes, collectively named the *Neutral Nation*, on
" account of their abstaining from taking any part in the
" wars of their neighbours, and preserving terms of amity
" with them all. The whole of the above-named tribes,
" viz: the *Micmacs* or *Souriquois*, *Etchemins*, *Abenaquis*,
" *Sokokis*, *Montagnais*, *Bull-heads* or *Attikamegues*, *Algon-*
" *quins*, *Nipissings*, *Ottawas*, *Chippewas*, *Foxes*, *Sacs*, *Meno-*
" *monees*, *Mascoutens*, *Kikapoos*, *Hurons* or *Wyandots*, *Tio-*
" *nontates* or *Petuns*, together with some other minor tribes
" south of Lake Erie, and extending to the valleys of the
" Ohio and the Mississipi are considered as belonging to or
" derived from the great *Algonquin* or *Algic* stock. On the
" south of the St. Lawrence, west of the river Richelieu,
" and extending southward and westward along the shores
" of Lake Ontario, were the principal settlements and
" hunting-grounds of the *Iroquois*, sometimes called *Huron-*

" *Iroquois*, the most famous of all the tribes of Indians con-
" cerned in the history of Canada and New England.   They
" consisted of five considerable tribes : the *Mohawks*, the
" *Oneidas*, the *Onondagas*, the *Cayugas*, and the *Senecas*, to
" whom were joined in the year 1712, the *Tuscaroras* from
" Carolina.   They formed the celebrated league or confede-
" racy of *Five Nations*, having their head-quarters in the
" north-eastern parts of the State of New York.   *   *   *
"   *   *   Before the coming of the French intense enmity
" and unceasing warfare had subsisted between the *Iroquois*
" and the Indians of Canada—more especially the *Hurons*,
" *Algonquins*, and *Abenaquis*, with whom it will be seen the
" French took part against the *Iroquois*."

Such were the wonderful people who once roamed over
this continent, a people differing alike from the barbarians
of the old world, and from what we might have expected
in the new, with dark lines thickly drawn perhaps but yet
with glimmerings of light and loftier possibilities, a people
destined as we shall see from a necessarily rapid sketch of
subsequent events to play a very prominent part in the history of our country.   Say you that they were blood-thirsty,
cruel, vindictive, barbarous ?   Perhaps they were, but
before condemning these savages too severely we must
turn our eyes towards countries professedly Christian,
and see what was going on there about the same time.
On the 24th August, 1572, just 37 years after Jacques
Cartier first cast anchor opposite the Indian village of
Stadacona, occurred in France the massacre of St. Bartholo-
mew, by which from 25,000 to 30,000 French subjects were
butchered in cold blood during three days.   In England, a
few years later we find people burned at the stake for hold-
ing, conscientiously, certain religious opinions ; and in the
same country in the following century, we have the
" Bloody Assizes " and the infamous Judge Jeffreys, a being whose atrocities were scarcely surpassed by any that

are recorded against the North American Indians. Indeed
very frequently the nobility of character is all on the side
of the Indian and the reverse on that of the White. They
were cruel because they were savage. They knew no
better. It was a point of honor with them to torture their
enemies; but, if they did inflict suffering on others they
were ready heroically to bear similar tortures themselves
if chance ordained it. The barbarities of the Inquisition
took place among Christians, and their parallel among
savages should not therefore excite much surprise.

THE INDIAN AND THE WHITE MAN.

Although the first contact of the white man with the
Indians of this country was not marked by the cruelties
which were practised elsewhere, one event occurred which
was not calculated to prepossess them in his favor, Jacques-
Cartier when re-embarking for France in the spring of
1536, having carried off with him by stratagem Donacona, the
Indian Chief at Stadacona, and several of his people, who
all died in that country shortly afterwards.

In 1608 Samuel de Champlain the first Governor of Quebec, landed on the present site of the city of that name.
He found the villages of Stadacona and Hochelaga, mentioned by Cartier, to have become extinct, owing no doubt to
the wars constantly being waged amongst the Indians
themselves. Colden reports that the Indians known as the
Five Nations, according to a tradition extant amongst themselves, once occupied the neighbourhood of Montreal, (the
site of the Indian village of Hochelaga) whence the Algonquins drove them. At the time of Champlain's arrival
just alluded to, a state of war existed between the *Algonquins* and *Hurons* on the one hand, and the *Five Nations*
on the other, and the former were desirous to obtain the
assistance of the Europeans in their favor. Champlain was
anxious to cultivate friendship with these nations, his

neighbours, in order to extend the fur trade, and to obtain their help in exploring the interior of the country, and in consequence he was readily induced to ally himself with them against the Iroquois or five Nations, a determination which cost his countrymen dearly in after times, as by it he voluntarily arrayed himself against a people who had not so far molested him, and whose implacable and deadly hate he thereby secured for more than a century.

This determination on Champlain's part resulted in his undertaking with the Algonquins and Hurons three expeditions against the Iroquois, in the first of which he made a successful attack on them in the vicinity of Lake George ; secondly, in the following year, he again attacked them successfully near the mouth of the Richelieu ; and thirdly in the summer of 1615, when the Hurons, Algonquins, and French were defeated by the Iroquois in the country of the latter south of Lake Ontario, a defeat which in its consequences proved highly disastrous to the vanquished Indian tribes, for the Iroquois waged war against them with slight intermission during the next thirty-five years, until they had destroyed all their settlements, and put an end to their existence as a distinct people.

The year 1615 was noted for the arrival of six Recollet Fathers, who visited the Hurons along with Champlain, one going next year amongst the Neutral Nation. In June, 1625, there arrived out five of the order of Jesuits, among whom were Charles Lallement and Jean de Breboeuf, destined to undergo a cruel death at the hands of the Indians in later years. These Jesuits, with others who followed them, exhibited a heroic persistency in the work of endeavouring to convert the Indians to Christianity, which the greatest hardships and the most horrid cruelties could not turn from its purpose. It fell to the lot of several of them to undergo the cruel tortures of the Indians, and

they surprised the latter by the determined courage with
which they bore them. In spite of torture and death the
mission was persisted in for about a quarter of a century,
till the destruction of the doomed Hurons by their enemies,
the Iroquois, necessarily ended it.

About this time too the traders at Tadousac and elsewhere began to supply the Indians with the "fire-water"
which has proved such a curse to them ever since.

In 1636 the Iroquois penetrated for the first time collectively into the midst of the Hurons, and a desultory warfare continued, the Iroquois also harrassing the newly
erected French establishment at Ville-Marie in 1643 and
1644. In 1645 a peace was made at Three Rivers between
the French and their allies on the one hand and the Oneida
canton of the Iroquois on the other, which however was
broken the following year, and then ensued the usual raids.
massacres, burnings and torturings of their Indian enemies
by the Iroquois, who were about this time being supplied
with fire-arms and ammunition by the Dutch residents of
what is now the State of New York. The colony of Mas-
sachusetts having in 1648 applied to the French with a
view to arranging for reciprocity of trade, the then French
Governor, D'Aillebout, sent a deputation to carry out their
views on condition that the New Englanders should aid
them in putting down the Iroquois. This the New
Englanders courteously refused, as the Iroquois had never
molested them ; and this overture on the part of the French
having become known to the Iroquois, they rushed to arms
with redoubled fury, with the purpose of exterminating
both the Canadian Indians and the French. At this time
the Hurons and Algonquins far outnumbered the Iroquois ;
indeed the Hurons alone were not much inferior in force,
for the strength of the five Iroquois nations is estimated to
have been now considerably less than three thousand war-

riors.. The superiority of the Iroquois lay in their better organization, better discipline. They now, in 1648, fell upon the establishment at Sillery, where four hundred families of converted Indians were settled It was Sunday morning, and most of the inhabitants were at church, when suddenly an indiscriminate slaughter was begun of men, women, and children, the priest himself, after receiving numerous blows, being thrown into the flames of the church. The village was also destroyed by fire. On the 4th of July, 1648, a body of Iroquois fell suddenly upon the village of St. Joseph, on the South-eastern frontier of the Huron country, and slaughtered every soul in the place to the number of seven hundred, including the priest, Père Antony Daniel: on 16th March, 1649, a similar fate befel the neighbouring settlement of St. Ignace, where about four hundred were killed ; and the next day the same band fell on the village of St. Louis, where most of the inhabitants were put to death, in many instances by torture, the Jesuits Brebœuf and Lallemant, who were in charge of the settlement, being subjected to the latter fate.

After some further hostilities, the Hurons, utterly defeated and disheartened, agreed with one accord to leave the country. A few reluctantly united with their conquerors, others found an asylum with other neighbouring tribes, and the rest sought refuge in the Island of St. Joseph, in Lake Huron. where famine and the Iroquois again decimated them, until at last a broken remnant of this once formidable nation besought their missionaries to convey them to Quebec, where they could be under the protection of the French, and accordingly, setting out by way of Lake Nipissing and the Ottawa Valley, headed by Père Ragueneau, they finally reached Quebec in 1650. Here they were joined the following year by about four hundred more. They were given land near the South-western extremity of the Island of Orleans. In 1656, however, the Iroquois again made a descent on them, and carried off a large number under the very guns of Quebec, after which calamity they were removed to Quebec, and lodged in a square enclosure of palisades close to the fort. Here they remained about ten years, when they were removed to Ste. Foye, and six years afterwards, when the soil was impoverished, and the wood in the neighbourhood exhausted, they again removed, under the auspices of the Jesuits, to Old Lorette, and before the end of the century they formed the village of Jeune Lorette, where their descendants can be found at the present time. The result of all was that not only the Huron countries, but those about the valley of the Ottawa, all teeming with population, as they had been, were become howling wildernesses.

The Iroquois, having disposed of the Hurons, turned their attention to the French settlements, until it was no longer safe for the colonists to go about their affairs without arms. They also now attacked the Neutral Nation, and in 1650 completely annihilated them. In 1653 they, of their own accord, sent deputies to make a peace with the French, which having been concluded, they took advantage of the opportunity, during the next ten years, to destroy successively the Eries, the Ottawas, and the Andastes, of the latter a small remnant only escaping, and the former leaving no trace of its existence but the great Lake which bears its name. The conquerors now held, it was reckoned, undisputed sway over a country five hundred miles in circuit. In 1670 a number of converted Iroquois migrated to Canada, and were located at first at La Prairie; subsequently as it was found that the soil was unsuited to the cultivation of their principal article of food, *maize*, they were removed to Sault St Louis (Caughnawaga) and lands assigned to them, which are occupied by their descendants to this day. A similar Iroquois settlement was made at Lake of the Two Mountains in the same vicinity.

Into the subsequent calamitous events we shall not now enter very fully. The succession of the English to the Dutch in New York, the boundary quarrels and border wars, the sickening array of murders, pillagings, and massacres, the butchery at Lachine by the Iroquois, and the terrible massacre at Schenectady, and, later on at Fort William Henry, both by the Canadian Indians, the capture of Quebec in 1759, and cession at Montreal the following year, the attempt on the colony in 1775 by the Americans, and the warfare waged by the same power in 1812, all followed in due succession.

The Iroquois, especially the Mohawks and Senecas, had been the firm allies originally of the Dutch, and after the taking of New York in 1664, of the English, and their alliance with the latter was never broken by any quarrels or warlike proceedings. They acted as a barrier between the British colonists and the French colonists on the North, and materially aided in sweeping away the chain of forts from the great Lakes down the Ohio and Mississippi valleys, by which it was hoped by the French to confine the British colonies to territory on the Atlantic seaboard. They were also present under Sir William Johnson at the capitulation at Montreal in 1760. But what was the cost to them of their long periods of war ? As early as 1660 their numbers are said to have been reduced to 2,200 warriors, of whom not more than 1,200 were of the true Iroquois stock. The rest were a mixture of adopted prisoners—Hurons. Neutrals, Eries, and Indians of various Algonquin tribes.

Were the Iroquois then more cruel and blood-thirsty than the other Indian tribes ? They can scarcely be so characterized. As respects ferocity of nature there was no appreciable difference between any of these tribes. The Iroquois, by their superior ability, their better organization, their quickness to learn lessons from experience, had succeeded in attaining the *power* of crushing their enemies, which they then proceeded to exercise. Had the Algonquins and Hurons succeeded in obtaining the upper hand over their adversaries, the Iroquois, there is no reason to suppose that the extermination of the latter would have been delayed, or that it would have been accomplished with one whit more humanity.

After the capitulation of 1760 many of the Indian tribes of the West, who had been in amicable relations with the French, were not pleased at the country being given up to the British. Nine-tenths of these Indians were still in the French interest. The Indians of Quebec had been glad to have the aid of the French in their contests with the Iroquois, and the Iroquois had looked to the English to protect them against the French. The French required no cessions of land, and in their trade and intercourse with the natives did not leave upon the minds of the latter the impression that they had come to permanently reside in the country, or that they were the vanguard of a people who would eventually spread themselves over the land and sweep from it its original owners. The Western Indians looked with great jealousy upon the evident design of the colonists in Virginia to cross the Alleghanies and open up a route for European immigration into the interior of the country, and they were anxious to have the aid of the French in opposing this design; whilst it suited the views of the latter power admirably that the Indians should be imbued with the desire to drive back the English. The Indians were amazed then at the downfall of French power in 1760; they were much dissatisfied with this result, and hoped to retrieve it; and from this dissatisfaction arose one of the most savage and prolonged wars, that of Pontiac in 1763. Pontiac was a great Indian war-chief, who was endowed with great courage, intelligence, and system. He formed a project similar to that which Tecumseh entertained some forty years afterwards. He united all the North-western tribes of Ottawas, Chippewas, and Pottowatamies in one great confederacy against the British, and planned a simultaneous attack on all the trading posts in their possession, and so far succeeded that ten of these forts were surprised about the same time, and all the English soldiers and traders massacred, whilst the French were spared. Pontiac afterwards laid siege to Detroit and kept it in a state of siege for twelve months; it was gallantly defended by Major Gladwyn, until relieved by Gen. Bradstreet with 3,000 men. The Indian tribes afterwards had to sue for peace, and Pontiac returned to Illinois, where he was afterwards murdered through private animosity by a Peoria Indian.

The opposition of Pontiac having been subdued, and the Indians having been shown, by a great display of military force, that the nation with which they had to deal was one capable of carrying out its behests, a new era dawned in the relations of these Indians with British authority, an era of greater sympathy, greater trustfulness; and in the inauguration of this better state of things the hand of a wise administrator was seen, to whose memory the nation owes much, the hand of the Superintendent-General of Indian affairs, Sir William Johnson, the beloved of the Iroquois. He, in 1764, arranged for a general convention of Indian tribes at Fort Niagara, where he collected 1,700 warriors, and prepared wise measures for a treaty of peace, amity, and alliance, which was afterwards extended to other tribes, and resulted in a general pacification, in which the following among other tribes joined: the Chippewas, Mississagies, Pottawattamies, Delawares, Shawanees and Miamies. He also took measures to regulate and place on a satisfactory footing all matters of Indian trade, and in his dealings with the tribes exhibited such a prudent, conciliatory spirit, combined with justice, firmness, and moderation, as to gradually gain over the good-will of the Indians, and lay the foundation for a more friendly feeling towards the British authorities, which has been growing and ripening ever since. It was indeed fortunate that the British authorities should choose as the chief of the Indian Department at this juncture so politic and judicious a man as Sir William Johnson, and should associate him with others, as subordinates, similarly minded.

At the time of the Revolutionary war a large proportion of the Western tribes took sides with the British. This was owing partly no doubt to a more friendly feeling having by this time sprung up. It was owing also to an idea that the British would come out most successfully in the struggle and a desire to be on the winning side; and also to a hope that the British would help them afterwards to confine the more Southern settlements to the territory to the East of the valley of the Ohio. The Iroquois, with slight exception, remained firm in their allegiance to Great Britain, their ancient ally, and suffered severely during the war, being defeated and driven out of their country by Gen. Sullivan. A portion of them, including the Mohawk tribe, afterwards came over to Canada, along with their famous chief Tyendinaga, better known as Col. Brant, and had lands granted them by the British Government where their descendants are to be found at the present day. The Revolutionary war sounded the death-knell of this celebrated league, and we do not hear of them as a body taking part in the next struggle. Their celebrated chief Tyendinaga, or Col. Brant, so-called from having held a lieut.-colonelcy in the British army, was a man of wonderful ability and skill. In his youth he had been a pupil at Dr. Wheelock's school; he was employed as an interpreter and translator at the missionary station at Fort Hunter, and was brother to the Indian wife of Sir William Johnson,

who was revered by the Iroquois as their leader and counsellor, and who conducted their affairs with such consum-
mate ability, and such benefit to British power. Brant
became the hero of the Iroquois, and at the time of the
Revolutionary war was very active on the side of the
British, for whom he had a very warm attachment, and
whose cause he served till the close of the war. The poet
Campbell, in his " Gertrude of Wyoming," gave him the
discredit of some acts of cruelty which were committed by
others. In the later editions of the work the charge is
withdrawn, it having been proved that Brant was not even
present.

In the war of 1812 a large proportion of the Westerly
Indian tribes took sides with the British. The great chief
Tecumseh was intimately connected with this war. He
was a Shawanee chief, and a valiant warrior, born in Ohio
in 1770. He is said from his earliest years to have given
evidence of the superior powers which afterwards characterized him. He had a high reputation for integrity ; his
word was inviolable. He has been described as " stamped
a hero by the hand of nature, and equally distinguished by
policy and eloquence." With the aid of his brother he had,
about the year 1804, conceived the idea of uniting all the
Western Indians in a confederacy, to make a simultaneous
attack upon the frontier settlements, in order to prevent
further encroachments on the Red man's territory. It is
difficult to say, of course, but yet it is just possible, that if
the United States had had a master-hand such as Sir
William Johnson at this time, Tecumseh might have been
prevented, through friendly intercession, from using his
great influence against them. Tecumseh proposed to
Governor Harrison that they should both go together to
Washington to lay before the President in person his grie-
vances on the land question, and ask the President's deci-
sion. This proposition the Governor refused. Tidings of

the proposed movement against the White settlements had been of course brought to Gen. Harrison, and it is supposed that deceptive information afterwards reached him to the effect that large numbers of Indians were assembling at Tippecanoe with hostile intent, and that it would be advisable to disperse them at once. He accordingly attacked the Indians at Tippecanoe, killing about 40 and wounding a like number. Exasperated by what they considered an unjustifiable outrage, the Indians were all the more ready to join the British in the war of 1812, which broke out shortly afterwards. Tecumseh was one of those who did so. Being importuned by the Americans to attend a council to try and arrange for the neutrality of the Indians in the struggle, he replied: " No, I have taken sides with " the British, and I will suffer my bones to bleach upon " this shore before I will recross that river to join in any " council of neutrality." He kept his word. In 1813 a battle was fought near Chatham, in which the Americans under General Harrison beat General Procter with considerable loss, and in this battle Tecumseh fell, pierced, it is said, by the bullets of Kentucky mounted riflemen whilst fighting bravely for the British at the head of his warriors.

THEIR PRESENT CONDITION

During the time that has since elapsed, down to the present day, the treatment of the Indians by our authorities has continued to be kind and just. Those who had been located on various tracts of land by the French (at Caughnawaga, &c.) have been protected in all their rights ; reserves have been apportioned to other tribes : wise regulations have been made for their government, and measures taken for their general improvement, which can be best judged of by looking at their fruits in the condition of the Indians to-day. All are contented and peaceful, and in one instance only do we find anything to the contrary, viz. : among the Indians at Oka, Lake of Two Mountains, and there the dispute is not with the Government, but with the

Seminary of St. Sulpice. These difficulties being now before the courts, we will not enter further into them here.

From the interesting report for 1876 of the Department of the Interior, the Deputy Superintendent-General of Indian affairs, and from other sources, we glean the following particulars :

The total number of Indians in the several provinces of the Dominion is as follows :—

Ontario	15,549
Quebec	10,804
	26,353
Nova Scotia	2,091
New Brunswick	1,440
Prince Edward Island	299
Manitoba, and the North-West territories.	25,945
British Columbia	32,020
Rupert's Land	4,370
	92,518

Of the above the

Six Nations of Grand River number	3,069
Mohawks, of the Bay of Quinté	822
Oneidas, of the Thames	604

Besides other scattered bodies.

These are remnants of those who supported the British cause during the revolutionary war, and afterwards migrated to Canada, and received grants of the land they now occupy in 1784.

Then there are the

Chippewas of Lake Superior		1,875
"	" Lake Huron	1,430
"	" Saugeen	341
"	" Cape Croker	380
"	" Snake Island	131
"	" Rama	257
"	" Christian Island	188
Chippewas and Pottawattamies of Sarnia		556
Chippewas and Munsees of the Thames		571
Chippewas, Ottawas, and Pottawattamies of Walpole Island		845
Wyandotts (or Hurons) of Anderdon		76
Manitoulin Island Indians		1,530

The latter, we presume, made up of different tribes.

Besides the above there are various other Indian settlements of different tribes or nations in the Province of Ontario.

In the Province of Quebec we have the

Iroquois of Caughnawaga		1,511
"	" St. Regis	947
Iroquois and Algonquins of the Lake of Two Mountains		506

These are descendants of the Indians converted to christianity by the early Jesuit Missionaries, and located on these lands by the French during their occupation of the country.

Then we have the

Hurons of Lorette, (of whom mention has been made previously)		295
Abenaquis of St. Francis		268
"	" Becancour	67

Micmacs of Maria.......................	67
" " Restigouche...........................	451
Montagnais of Lake St. John............	245
" " Moisie, Seven Islands, Bet-	
siamits, and Mingan............	1.300
Naskapees of Lower St. Lawrence.......... ..	2,800
Algonquins, Nipissings, Ottawas, of the	
Ottawa and St. Maurice districts, &c.,	
&c., about......	800

Besides members of various tribes scattered in different parts of the Province.

In the Maritime Provinces the Indians are chiefly Micmacs.

There are of Indian pupils attending school :—

In Ontario............	1,857
In Quebec	394

Of course the chief difficulties to contend with in dealing with the Indian are his constitutional indolence, his natural antipathy to any fixed residence or employment, and his partiality for the "fire-water," a taste which seems to have become ingrained in him ever since he first learned from the white man the use of a beverage which has proved such a curse to both. It is gratifying to know that in each of these particulars an improvement on the whole sure, if slow, is visible, and that with the supervision and watchfulness exercised by the authorities, a gradual advance is likely in each generation, until at last the Indian, instead of being a member of a barbarous, heathen horde, wandering aimlessly over this vast continent, will have attained to the proud position of an enfranchised christian citizen of the first christian nation in the world.

It is generally believed that in these older provinces the Indian race is, from one cause or another, gradually waning and becoming extinct. This idea is erroneous; the Indian population is rather on the increase in the older provinces, with the exception of Prince Edward's Island.

The revenue which flows into the Indian fund of the Dominion, year by year, is of two classes, viz.: that which is derived from the sale of land, timber, stone, and so forth, and which is placed to the credit of *Capital* account; and that derived from interest accruing on invested capital, from legislative grants, rents, fines, &c., which is distributed semi-annually amongst the individuals belonging to the various tribes in the Provinces of Ontario and Quebec. The gross sum standing, on the 30th June, 1876, at the credit of the capital account of the various Trust Funds, which belong exclusively to, and are employed for the benefit of the Indians of Ontario and Quebec, was $2,923,335.17, as against $2,884,972.44 on the 30th June, 1875, showing an increase of $38,362.73 since the 1st July, 1875. The interest which accrued during the same period amounted to $155,928.71. This last sum has been in part expended for the benefit of, and in part distributed among the various bands in whose interest the investments were made.

The funds employed in the Indian service in the Provinces of Nova Scotia, New Brunswick, Prince Edward Island, British Columbia, Manitoba, and in the North-West Territories, are provided by Legislative appropriations, with the exception of certain insignificant amounts, in the case of some of those Provinces, which have accumulated from the sale or lease of small tracts of land, or from timber dues.

The average attendance at the Indian schools of such as are of an age to attend is not found as large as desirable.

Of all the Indian tribes those of Ontario are the most civilized and prosperous. The value of the personal property of the Ontario Indians is said to average $20.75 per capita; of their real estate, $385.93; and of invested capital, $210.00; giving an actual value per capita for every Indian in Ontario of $616.68. About one-third of their number are children, and of these about a third attend school. The value of the real estate belonging to them has been much enhanced by the general prosperity of the Province, and the growth of towns and villages in the vicinity of the various reserves.

The Six Nation Indians of Grand River are settled upon a Reserve of some 52,000 acres of cleared and uncleared land; they have a prosperous agricultural society, and a fair stock of horses, oxen, cows, &c. They are christians of various denominations, except about 800 pagans, who do not appear disposed to abandon the ceremonies of their fathers. In regard to education, the departmental report says:—" The good work of the New England Company is zealously prosecuted by the reverend missionaries, and by means of eight Primary Schools under their superintendence, and that most excellent ' Mohawk Institute,' in charge of Mr. Ashton; also, by the Wesleyan Conference through their missionary and two schools; and the creditable example of the Mississiguas who maintain two schools, in striking contrast with the apathy of the Six Nations, who still fail in their duty, because having always been provided with schools, they have thought it unnecessary to contribute towards their support: they appear of late to be more sensible, that they must now aid in the cause of education. Mr. Ashton, the Superintendent of the Mohawk Institute, reports 83 pupils in course of instruction, who, while there, are supported and clothed at the expense of the Company, and taught the ordinary branches and vocal music; the boys work a farm of 300 acres; the girls do the house-work, including baking of bread and making the clothing of the pupils. The statute labor is generally well done, the people desirous of good roads through their Reserve, while the Council votes moneys for both roads and bridges. Drunkenness has diminished, and the temperance cause is promoted by several native societies; whilst the severity of the recent law against selling or giving liquor to Indians has had a good effect."

The Mohawks of the Bay of Quinté are reported to be improving in habits of industry, and generally support their families in comfort. The Chippewas of Saugeen are said to be making fair progress in industrial habits. Letters have been received at Ottawa from the more intelligent of them, enquiring as to enfranchisement provided for them under the recent Indian Act, the provisions of which seem to have afforded much satisfaction. Of other bands similar satisfactory reports are made. Many are employed hunting, trading, maple-sugar making, carrying goods in their boats for traders, &c., the women manufacturing basket-work and the like, and all in as good circumstances as can be expected, and with as good opportunities for advancement as it is possible for the Government to secure to them.

In the Province of Quebec the total value of the property (of all kinds) of the Indians is $165 per head. About 400 children attend school.

At Caughnawaga the men are chiefly engaged in navigating steamers and rafts over the Lachine rapids; some cultivate land, and others voyage to the United States. The women are chiefly occupied in bead-work. The tribe have profited somewhat by the lease of a valuable stone quarry within their reserve to certain contractors in Montreal. In spite of repeated fines imposed for the sale of intoxicating liquor in the place, the Indians are still able to get it, and grave disorders consequently arise. The Indians of the Lake of Two Mountains are chiefly engaged in agriculture; some voyage to the North-west. The chief occupation of the women is bead-work. The St. Regis Indians are employed in rafting and boating as pilots and hands; cultivating, hunting, making baskets, bead-work, &c. They do not take much interest in the schooling of their children. The Abenaquis of St. Francis are *voyageurs* to a large extent. The Indians of Lake St. John are improving. They are poor, partly owing to the high prices of provisions, dry goods, &c., and because they get less for their furs than is paid at posts whence the transport is less expensive.

The Indians of Nova Scotia are generally sober and industrious. Their property (real and personal estate) is rated at $25.50 per head. Out of 381 children 80 attend school. Coopering and fishing are the chief employments.

In New Brunswick the value of their property is about $217 per head. They have no schools, and employ themselves little with agriculture.

The Prince Edward Island Indians have no reserve from the Crown, their lands being set apart through the benevolence of the Aborigines' Protection Society and of private individuals. They hold real and personal estate to the value of about $24 per head; they have not made much progress.

The Indian Act.

Turning now to the Indian Act of 1876, from which such beneficial results are expected, and which of course applies to all portions of the Dominion, we will examine certain of its provisions. In regard to the protection of reserves, section II provides that :

"No person, or Indian other than an Indian of the band, shall settle, reside or hunt upon, occupy or use any land or marsh, or shall settle, reside upon or occupy any road, or allowance for roads running through any reserve belonging to or occupied by such band; and all mortgages or hypothecs given or consented to by any Indian, and all leases, contracts and agreements made or purporting to be made by any Indian, whereby persons or Indians other than Indians of the band are permitted to reside or hunt upon such reserve, shall be absolutely void."

The next following sections provide for the removal, by the authorities, of any person (white man or Indian) so trespassing, and for his incarceration in gaol should he return after the first removal: they also provide penalties for any one removing unlawfully from a reserve any timber, stone, mineral, or other article of value.

No reserve or portion of a reserve can be sold, alienated, or leased, untill it has been released or surrendered to the crown for the purposes of this Act, and no such release and surrender shall be valid without the assent of the majority of the band in council assembled.

The next sections provide for the punishment of any agent giving false information in regard to land, or hindering any person from bidding upon or purchasing lands offered at public sale.

Sections 59 and 60 are as follows :—

"The Governor in Council may, subject to the provisions of this Act, direct how, and in what manner, and by whom the moneys arising from sales of Indian lands, and from the property held or to be held in trust for the Indians, or from any timber on Indian lands or reserves, or from any other source for the benefit of Indians (with the exception of any small sum not exceeding ten per cent. of the proceeds of any lands, timber or property, which may be agreed at the time of the surrender to be paid to the members of the band interested therein), shall be invested from time to time, and how the payments or assistance to which the Indians may be entitled shall be made or given, and may provide for the general management of such moneys, and direct what percentage or proportion thereof shall be set apart from time to time, to cover the cost of and attendant upon the management of reserves, lands, property and moneys under the provisions of this Act, and for the construction or repair of roads passing through such reserves or lands, and by way of contribution to schools frequented by such Indians.

The proceeds arising from the sale or lease of any Indian lands, or from the timber, hay, stone, minerals or other valuables thereon, or on a reserve, shall be paid to the Receiver General to the credit of the Indian fund."

The portion of the Act having reference to intoxicants is properly very stringent :—

" Whoever sells, exchanges with, barters, supplies or gives to any Indian, or non treaty Indian in Canada, any kind of intoxicant, or causes or procures the same to be done, or connives or attempts thereat, or opens or keeps, or causes to be opened or kept, on any reserve or special reserve, a tavern, house or building where any intoxicant is sold, bartered, exchanged or given, or is found in possession of any intoxicant in the house, tent, wigwam or place of abode of any Indian or non-treaty Indian, shall, on conviction thereof before any judge, stipendiary magistrate or two justices of the peace, upon the evidence of one credible witness other than the informer or prosecutor, be liable to imprisonment for a period not less than one month nor exceeding six months, with or without hard labor, and be fined not less than fifty nor more than three hundred dollars, with costs of prosecution,—one moiety of the fine to go to the informer or prosecutor, and the other moiety to Her Majesty, to form part of the fund for the benefit of that body of Indians or non-treaty Indians, with respect to one or more members of which the offence was committed: and the commander or person in charge of any steamer or other vessel, or boat, from or on board of which any intoxicant has been sold, bartered, exchanged, supplied or given to any Indian or non-treaty Indian, shall be liable, on conviction thereof before any judge, stipendiary magistrate or two justices of the peace, upon the evidence of one credible witness other than the informer or prosecutor, to be fined not less than fifty nor exceeding three hundred dollars for each such offence, with costs of prosecution,—the moieties of the fine to be applicable as hereinbefore mentioned; and in default of immediate payment of such fine and costs any person so fined shall be committed to any common gaol, house of correction, lock-up, or other place of confinement by the judge, stipendiary magistrate or two justices of the peace before whom the conviction has taken place, for a period of not less than one nor more than six months, with or without hard labor, or until such fine and costs are paid ; and any Indian or non-treaty Indian who makes or manufactures any intoxicant, or who has in his possession, or concealed, or who sells, exchanges with, barters, supplies or gives to any other Indian or non-treaty Indian in Canada any kind of intoxicant shall, on conviction thereof, before any judge, stipendiary magistrate or two justices of the peace, upon the evidence of one credible witness other than the informer or prosecutor, be liable to imprisonment for a period of not less than one month nor more than six months, with or without hard labor; and in all cases arising under this section, Indians or non-treaty Indians, shall be competent witnesses: but no penalty shall be incurred in case of sickness where the intoxicant is made use of under the sanction of a medical man or under the directions of a minister of religion."

Provision is also made for the forfeiture of any keg, barrel, or other receptacle in which such liquor has been contained ; and the punishment, by fine or imprisonment, of the Indian or other person in whose possession such keg, &c., may be found.

The Act then goes on to provide that boats or other vessels used in conveying intoxicants, in contravention of this Act, shall be subject to seizure and forfeiture; that articles exchanged for intoxicants may be seized and forfeited; that Indians intoxicated may be arrested and imprisoned until sober, and fined, and further punished if they refuse to say from whom they got the intoxicants.

The provision for the enfranchisement of the Indians is important:

"Whenever any Indian man, or unmarried woman, of the full age of twenty-one years, obtains the consent of the band of which he or she is a member to become enfranchised, and whenever such Indian has been assigned by the band a suitable allotment of land for that purpose, the local agent shall report such action of the band, and the name of the applicant to the Superintendent-General; whereupon the said Superintendent-General, if satisfied that the proposed allotment of land is equitable, shall authorize some competent person to report whether the applicant is an Indian who, from the degree of civilization to which he or she has attained, and the character for integrity, morality and sobriety which he or she bears, appears to be qualified to become a proprietor of land in fee simple; and upon the favorable report of such person, the Superintendent-General may grant such Indian a location ticket as a probationary Indian, for the land allotted to him or her by the band.

Any Indian who may be admitted to the degree of Doctor of Medicine, or to any other degree by any University of Learning, or who may be admitted in any Province of the Dominion to practice law either as an Advocate or as a Barrister or Counsellor or Solicitor or Attorney, or to be a Notary Public, or who may enter Holy Orders or who may be licensed by any denomination of Christians as a Minister of the Gospel, shall *ipso facto* become and be enfranchised under this Act.

After the expiration of three years (or such longer period as the Superintendent-General may deem necessary in the event of such Indian's conduct not being satisfactory), the Governor may, on the report of the Superintendent-General, order the issue of letters patent, granting to such Indian in fee simple the land which had, with this object in view, been allotted to him or her by location ticket."

Provision is also made for the payment to the enfrancised Indian of his or her share of the funds at the credit of the band, and it is also ordered that the sections of the Act relating to enfranchisement shall not apply to any band of Indians in the Province of British Columbia, the Province of Manitoba, the North-West Territories, or the Territory of Keewatin, save in so far as the said sections may, by proclamation of the Governor-General, be from time to time extended, as they may be, to any band of Indians in any of the said Provinces or Territories.

THE NORTH-WEST.

Coming now to the North-West Territories, which are of greater interest at the present time. We have seen the conduct of the authorities towards the Indians nearer home and from it we may gather a fair idea of the course of gradual development which may be expected in those far-off regions. The Dominion of Canada no doubt succeeded to a careful and paternal Government in that country. The North-West Co. and the Hudson's Bay Co., which united in 1821, had charters by which the exclusive right of trade with the Indians in furs was granted them. They represented British authority, and had general jurisdiction in the country. There is little doubt that they might have made much trouble for themselves if their conduct towards the Indians had been marked by injustice or oppression, for we read that the trade was carried on throughout vast regions far from all control of law, and inhabited by savage races numbering about 150,000, divided into 40 or 50 tribes who were very easily prompted to deeds of violence. But the Company took a different course; they made the most laudable efforts to instruct and civilize, and finding the baneful effects of spirits, which were at first dealt in, they immediately with-held them as an article of trade.

On the Southern border of British Territory, extending from Red River to the Rocky Mountains, there were other tribes more fierce and warlike, subsisting chiefly by the chase of the Buffalo. Amongst the principal tribes were the Assineboines, Piegans, Blackfeet, Blood, Sarsee, and Plain Cree Indians.

In an article that has appeared in the March number of the *Atlantic Monthly*, attributed to a respected citizen of the United States at present residing amongst us, it is contended that the most warlike and self-reliant tribes, the Buffalo-hunters bold and fierce, were residents of the United States, and that on the Canada side the Indians were the gentle and quiet savages of a cold climate and fish diet, mere trappers of musk-rats and beavers, and this is given as one reason for Canada's success with the Indians. No doubt we have had the trappers of musk-rats and beavers, but we think it will be admitted, considering the six Buffalo-hunting tribes just mentioned, that we at least had our share of the latter on the British side, to say nothing of an importation from the United States in 1875, of Sioux, to whom we had to give nearly 15,000 acres of our land. These Sioux have behaved well since coming to our Territory, and so have the more recent importation under Sitting Bull up to the present time.

It is not the intention of this paper to discuss the American system of Indian management, or to make any invidious comparisons, but as the article just referred to deals with both Canadian and American systems in their relation to each other it may be permissible to pause here and summarize it in order to give one set of views in regard to the Indian question, quoting afterwards an article from a New York paper which deals with causes and effects from a different point of view, and one from which we have been more in the habit of regarding the matter in this country.

The writer of the article proceeds to argue that the French were more adaptable than the English, and less proud and exacting, mixed more with the natives, and made but little show of taking hold of the country; they erected trading-posts or forts throughout the country which became points of contact between the Colonists and Indians, resulting in a semi-civilization of the latter. In addition, they intermarried, and the short term of a generation was sufficient to establish a race of half-breeds who constituted a link between the new and old races, a natural bond of peace. When the English took Canada they took it as the French had thus made it, and chiefly got the good-will of the Indians in the transfer, of which they availed themselves in the war of the revolution immediately afterwards. The United States on the other hand took all the old English quarrels and ill-will of the Indians off their hands, with the enmity towards them which had grown up under the French *regime* added. They (the United States) had entailed on them the pernicious system of treaties with *tribes* as independent nations, buying sovereignty of them and paying them annuities. Whatever there was of system in the English dealing with the Indians they continued, under the disadvantage of comparison with the French system and with French facilities as practised in Canada. It is true the French had wars with the Indians, but they were with tribes south of the St. Lawrence. Canada has been free from border wars nearly all her existence, whilst the States have had a continued fight of two hundred years. The Hudson's Bay Co. has also been useful in facilitating the management of the Indians of Canada, and the reduction of the Indians of all the older Provinces to civilization has uniformerly succeeded a long acquaintance with the whites in trade. At present the Canadians maintain an armed force between the border and the Rocky Mountains, but it is a Mounted Police to govern the Indians, and not an army to protect the frontier. Instead of an army of occupation, which involves a state of war with the savages, as the United States actually have, the Canadians give their armed force the character of a constabulary, which presupposes peace and authority, so that instead of fighting the Indians they are ruling them. There is a prevailing impression that the United States Government is greatly at

fault in dealing with the Indians, and the fact that
the Canadians have so little trouble with them has led many
to suppose that they have some sovereign method that the
States should hasten to adopt, but the truth is that the
English are reaping where the French sowed good seed on
moderately good ground, whilst the Americans are reaping
where the English sowed dragon's teeth on wild soil. The
writer goes on to deal with the Indian policy of the two
countries, and says that the United States cannot adopt the
policy of Canada—even if it were perfect—which it is not,
as it will not apply, because one country has to do with a
people tame, practical, and at peace ; the other, with numerous tribes of fierce, impracticable, and independent
savages at war, and inspired by the spirit of recent battles.
" Before we can manage them" says the writer, " their
" tribal organizations must be broken up, their habits of
" life changed, they must be dismounted from their horses,
" and taught the gentler pursuits of herdsmen and led into
" occupations that will sustain them, and remove their
" present inducements to rob and plunder ; they must learn
" to depend upon honest industry and honest traffic, before
" we reach the point where the Canadians have their
" Indians."

The above is, we think, a fair summary of the arguments
advanced. There is no doubt the French did suit themselves more to the ways of the Indians, and their design of
occupying the country was not so apparent, except perhaps
to the Iroquois, who saw clearly that the French coveted
their country to the south of the lakes. The half-breeds too
exerted a beneficial influence. Still, the relations between
the English colonists and the Iroquois were quite as cordial
and sincere as those between the French and their Indians.
When the English took Canada they did not immediately
obtain the good-will of the Indians, witness the war of
Pontiac, but they cultivated that good-will subsequently

with considerable success. The Hudson's Bay Co. have of course been useful in facilitating the management of the Indians of this country, but that company represented British sovereignty, and established wise regulations, the absence of which might have entailed a different state of things. It is not quite correct to say our Mounted Police force is intended to govern the Indians : it is intended to govern both Whites and Indians, the former quite as much as the latter.

No doubt there are deplorable quarrels with, and outrages against the Indian, to be credited to the early colonists, for which the British must take their full share of blame up to the time of the Declaration of Independence, merely feeling thankful that since that era the abuses in the treatment of these original owners of the soil have, like other abuses, passed away ; still on the other hand there is a very strong and widespread opinion that the Indian troubles from which the people of the United States are now suffering are the outcome of " dragon's teeth," sown at a later date than that at which the British were responsible for the management of affairs in that country ; being sown in fact even in our own day by border ruffians and white savages who systematically violate all treaties with the Indians, and by dishonest agents who plunder them. These individuals, after having so exasperated the Indians as to lead them to take up arms against the whole white population, seem to save themselves by leaving the neighbourhood, whilst the U. S. troops, upon arriving and finding the Indians engaged in active hostilities against the white settlers, of course endeavour to punish them, and this is commonly the prelude to a general Indian war, in which valuable lives are lost, and much bitter feeling is engendered amongst the Indians against the Whites, and as a consequence against the Government. The real culprits—those *white savages*, who were the original cause of the trouble, have in the meantime escaped, and do not seem to suffer any of the serious consequences of the crimes they have committed.

The concluding portion of the article is doubtless correct ; it will have to come to this in time. The writer however does not say how the result he portrays is to be arrived at ; whether by the law of the sword, or of kindness.

We will now quote an article on this subject from a New York paper reviewing the report of the Commissioner of Indian affairs for 1877, and advocating a remedial system, which is almost identical with that now in force in this country :—

" The Indians and their Treatment.—We have received the annual report of the Commissioner of Indian Affairs for the year 1877, and observe that he has no difficulty in determining the cause of our troubles with the Indians. The cure for them which he prescribes will equally commend itself to the minds of all well-disposed persons. What are his remedies ? Here are some of them : A code of laws for the Indian reservations, with an Indian police for their enforcement. The giving of small farms to Indian families, thus fostering industrial habits among them. The introduction among them of the common school system, and the encouragement of missionary work to reclaim them from debasing paganism. A wise economy in feeding and clothing them, that idleness and pauperism may be discouraged and their opposites promoted. Evidently these are the agencies which, if promptly and wisely used, would go far to solve the Indian problem and prevent our periodical wars with the original natives of the soil. Unquestionably it would be well to have good laws and a police force among the Indians, but we are not to forget that the proper enforcement of laws upon the white transgressors who violate our treaties with the red man should be first inaugurated. The man who is severe with his own faults and those of his family will not often be involved in quarrels with neighbors. A proper administration at home always works well outwardly.

Then again the question comes up and will not be silenced : Are we, the party of the first part, although professing to be civilized and educated, more faithful in the observance of contracts and bargains than the Indians ? Many will agree with us that disinterested parties would probably render a verdict in favor of the savage. The report says that these men are employed as scouts by the army and found altogether faithful. They can be trusted. As much cannot be said of all white men. The Commissioner repeats a well known fact when saying that adults are less hopeful cases than the younger Indians. We must therefore begin with the young if we would build strongly and permanently, and this glorious work belongs pre-eminently to the churches of America, and should this very year be entered upon with fourfold more teachers and money. The suggestion is made that these people could easily be induced to engage largely in the cattle business, for which many of them exhibit considerable aptitude. Reading this report we are further impressed with the conviction that all our Indian wars are of our own creation, because of the rascalities and inhumanities, not of all, but of a number of the agents, and nearly all the traders. This is the root of the evil. These traders and agents value the dollar more than human blood. Vigorous justice upon them is an important part of the case, and we suggest that reform in our administration of Indian affairs begin with the white offender. It is a national disgrace that the aborigines of the country are too often left to the tender mercies of haughty and heartless, perhaps licentious, army officers and traders. We like to record to the credit of the North American Indian what many of the rising generation may not know, namely, that no Indian ever lifted his arm against the Quakers. Does not this prove beyond all cavil the conciliatory power of honest dealings and kind words. Scornful language and deeds of violence are dangerous boomerangs. They are like the curses that come home to roost. Unprincipled adventurers have won some money in the Black Hills and elsewhere, but the nation has to foot big bills as the result of our Indian wars. Have we not gone far enough on that thorny and costly, and above all, God condemned road?"

The Chicago *Tribune* also pays the following flattering compliment to Canada and its Government :—

" It speaks well for the efficiency of the Canadian system of dealing with Indians that the Government can safely and without protest distribute arms and ammunition among the tribes. In pursuance of a treaty made with the Blackfeet, forty-six of the Chiefs and head men of the tribe have each been furnished a Winchester rifle and 400 cartridges. The United States has not progressed so far as this in the science of getting along smoothly with its Indian wards." *

---

* NOTE.—Since this paper was written, the following items of information have appeared in the public press, and may well be annexed as illustrating the subject :—

THE PROVOCATIONS TO THE INDIANS.—The San Francisco *Call* of June 23 says: " In a formal interview by some white people, interpreters being present, the Bannock chiefs complain that they have been provoked to hostilities by the lies, frauds, and outrages practised on them by their Agent, Reinhart. He made them work, promised them pay, and refused to keep his promises. He ' starved, abused them, and lied to them.' This is all corroborated by Piute witnesses, who are friendly with the whites. Having profited by his frauds and lies, the Agent, well knowing what the consequences would be, saved his own scalp by getting out of the way in time ; and now innocent settlers, taken without warning and without any knowledge of the provocation, men, women, and children, scattered over a region twice as large as the State of Ohio, are paying the penalty of the rascally Agent's crimes with their lives and property. Amid the agonizing shrieks of the helpless victims of savage warfare, and the smoke that ascends from their burning houses, the real instigator of the war is obscured from the public eye, and only the Indians are thought of and sought to be punished as the criminals. The frauds and lies of the unprincipled Agent, after causing the cruel sacrifice of scores of innocent lives and some millions to the people and Treasury, will be glossed over and forgotten, and he will never be punished. His success in getting away with some thousands of dollars worth of plunder will encourage other scamps of Agents to imitate his example and cause

But, to return to the North-West. The Dominion Government, on taking over the country proceeded to establish law and order upon a sure and satisfactory foundation, and finding that bands of outlaws from the United States had established posts in these territories, where they sold arms, ammunition and spirituous liquors, and completely demoralized the tribes, the Government established the Mounted Police force, a body which has effectually eradicated the evils complained of, and has obtained, by its good conduct, strict discipline, thorough impartiality, and excellent management, a very high place in the respect and regard of the native tribes. So much so indeed, that as a recent reverend visitor to this province said life and property are now as safe in that territory as in our largest cities, and perhaps we may add safer than in *some* cities.

One serious difficulty which is looming up in the near future for the Indians of the North-West is the decrease in number of the buffalo. Until lately the Indian could

---

other tribes to revolt and burn, kill and destroy, as the Bannocks are doing this year, as the Nez Percés did last, as the Sioux did the year before that, and the Cheyennes at an earlier date. It would be a just and wise law that would hang any Indian Agent or Superintendent whose frauds or stealings instigate a tribe to acts of war and murder.''

How the Indians are Robbed.—A despatch from Fort Thompson, Dakota, dated July 11th, says Indian Commissioner Hoyt dropped on the Crow Agency on that date without notice. He obtained the books and papers of Indian Inspector Hammond, and discovered frauds and robbery unheard of even in Indian Agencies. Dr. Livingston is Agent at Crow Creek, and he and agent Craven at Cheyenne, and Gregory, at Lower Brule, have been conspirators together. The robberies of the Indians are traced back to 1870. They built a hotel at the Government's expense, and supplied it with beef, potatoes, milk, grain and hay from the Government warehouse. Livingston was a partner with Indian trader Hudson, whom he supplied with Indian Goods, which were sold to the Indians; he drew pay and rations for three hundred Indians more than were at his agency. Livingston owns a controlling interest in three silver mines in Nevada, about all the real property in Yankton, and has gratified his piety by presenting stained glass windows and marble fonts to churches. His agency as well as the others, have been seized. The ring threaten Hammond's life for exposing them. Gen. Hammond has superseded the agents at Crow Creek, Brule and Cheyenne by army officers.

count upon a practically unlimited supply of food from the immense herds of these animals which roamed over the prairie, and their skins were also very valuable to him both for his own use in various ways, and for purposes of traffic. For the last ten years, however, the numbers of the buffalo have been steadily diminishing, partly owing to indiscriminate slaughter on the part of the Whites and Half-breeds. and it is calculated that in another decade of years, unless prompt remedial measures are taken, the buffalo, as a source of supply of food, will be extinct. The Indians, to whom the buffalo hitherto has been indispensable, naturally regard this state of affairs with great alarm, and ask how they are to find subsistence when the buffalo is destroyed? His Honor Lieut.-Governor Morris recommended that a few simple regulations be made relating to the hunting and killing of the buffalo, and in this way he was satisfied that the herds could be preserved for many years, and we believe legislative action has been already taken on this subject. There seems however to be no doubt that wise precautions of this nature will only delay, not prevent, the ultimate extinction of the buffalo, and the authorities recognize the importance of preparing the native tribes for the time when unfortunately this result will supervene. This can only be done by encouraging the Indians to turn their attention to agriculture and other industrial pursuits, and it is satisfactory that as a rule they seem to be very desirous of obtaining the knowledge necessary to enable them to do so to advantage. His Honor Governor Morris, than whom we shall not desire better authority, states in speaking of the Indians of the Saskatchewan that, " he was surprised to find so great a willing- " ness on the part of the Indians to cultivate the soil, and " so great a desire to have their children instructed. The " Indians are tractable and docile : the universal demand " is for teachers, and for persons to instruct them how to " cultivate the ground and to build houses." In Manitoba the Indians have in several instances commenced the cultivation of the soil, and built houses for themselves.

There have been six treaties made between our Government and the Indians of the North-West, and if we note with satisfaction the confidence and evident good-will with which the latter entered into the treaties, we cannot but admire also the just and conciliatory spirit exhibited by the former in negotiating them.

Treaty No. 1 with the Chippewa and Swampy Cree Tribes of Indians was made on 3rd August, 1871. By it these tribes made over to Her Majesty and her successors for ever a certain tract of land specially designated, and Her Majesty agrees and undertakes to lay aside and reserve for the sole and exclusive use of the Indians certain other tracts, sufficient to furnish 160 acres for each family of five, or in that proportion for larger or smaller families. Her Majesty binds herself to maintain a school on each reserve when desired by the Indians, and to exclude intoxicating liquor.

" And with a view to show the satisfaction of Her Majesty with the behavior and good conduct of Her Indians, parties to this Treaty, She hereby, through Her Commissioner, makes them a present of five dollars for each Indian man, woman and child belonging to the Bands here represented.

Her Majesty's Commissioner shall, as soon as possible after the execution of this Treaty, cause to be taken an accurate census of all the Indians inhabiting the District above described, distributing them in families, and shall in every year ensuing the date hereof, at some period during the month of July, in each year, to be duly notified to the Indians, and at or near the respective reserves, pay to each Indian family of five persons the sum of fifteen dollars Canadian currency, or in like proportion for a larger or smaller family, such payment to be made in such articles as the Indians shall require of Blankets, clothing, prints (assorted colors), twine or traps, at the current cost price in Montreal, or otherwise, if Her Majesty shall deem the same desirable in the interests of Her Indian people, in cash.

And the undersigned Chiefs do hereby bind and pledge themselves and their people strictly to observe this Treaty, and to maintain perpetual peace between themselves and Her Majesty's white subjects, and not to interfere with the property or in any way molest the persons of Her Majesty's white or other subjects.

In witness whereof Her Majesty's said Commissioner and the said Indian Chiefs have hereunto subscribed and set their hand and seal, at the Lower Fort Garry, this day and year herein first above mentioned."

Here follow the names.

Treaty No. 2, made on 21st August, 1871, with the Chippewa Tribe, is similar in purport to the foregoing.

Treaty No. 3, ratified on 3rd October, 1873, with the Saulteaux Tribe of the Ojibbeway Indians, to the number of about 2,700, cedes a certain described tract of land embracing an area of about 55,000 square miles, and reserves are set apart in the proportion of one square mile to each family of five. Twelve dollars are presented to each man, woman, and child, in extinguishment of all claims preferred, and after a census has been taken Five Dollars are to be paid yearly to each Indian person, and fifteen hundred dollars are also to be annually expended by Her Majesty in the purchase of ammunition and twine for nets for the use of the Indians.

The Indians are still to have the right to pursue their avocations of hunting and fishing throughout the tract surrendered subject to regulations, and excepting such tracts as may from time to time be required for settlement, &c., by the Dominion Government or any of the subjects thereof duly authorized.

"It is further agreed between Her Majesty and the said Indians that the following articles shall be supplied to any Band of said Indians who are now actually cultivating the soil, or who shall hereafter commence to cultivate the land, that is to say—two hoes for every family actually cultivating; also one spade per family as aforesaid; one plough for every ten families as aforesaid; five harrows for every twenty families as aforesaid; one scythe for every family as aforesaid; and also one axe and one cross-cut saw, one hand saw, one pit saw, the necessary files, one grindstone, one augur for each Band, and also for each Chief for the use of his Band, one chest of ordinary carpenter's tools; also for each Band, enough of wheat, barley, potatoes and oats to plant the land actually broken up for cultivation by such Band; also for each Band, one yoke of oxen, one bull and four cows; all the aforesaid articles to be given once for all for the encouragement of the practice of agriculture among the Indians.

It is further Agreed between Her Majesty and the said Indians, that each Chief, duly recognized as such, shall receive an annual salary of twenty-five dollars per annum, and each subordinate officer, not exceeding three for each band, shall receive fifteen dollars per annum; and each such Chief and subordinate officer as aforesaid shall also receive, once in every three years, a suitable suit of clothing; and each Chief shall receive, in recognition of the closing of the treaty, a suitable flag and medal.

And the undersigned Chiefs, on their own behalf and on behalf of all other Indians inhabiting the tract within ceded, do hereby solemnly promise and engage to strictly observe this treaty, and also to conduct and behave themselves as good and loyal subjects of Her Majesty the Queen. They promise and engage that they will, in all respects, obey and abide by the law ; that they will maintain peace and good order between each other, and also between themselves and other tribes of Indians, and between themselves and others of Her Majesty's subjects, whether Indians or Whites, now inhabiting or hereafter to inhabit any part of the said coded tract ; and that they will not molest the person or property of any inhabitant of such coded tract, or the property of Her Majesty the Queen, or interfere with or trouble any person passing or travelling through the said tract or any part thereof; and that they will aid and assist the officers of Her Majesty in bringing to justice and punishment any Indian offending against the stipulations of this treaty, or infringing the laws in force in the country so ceded.

IN WITNESS WHEREOF, Her Majesty's said Commissioners and the said Indian Chiefs have hereunto subscribed and set their hands, at the North-West Angle of the Lake of the Woods, this day and year herein first above-named."

Treaty No. 4 was concluded on 15th September, 1874, between Her Majesty represented by Her Commissioners, Hon. Alexander Morris, Lieut.-Governor of Manitoba and the North-West Territories, the Hon. David Laird, then Minister of the Interior, and William Joseph Christie, Esq., of Brockville and the Cree, Saulteaux, and other Indians, inhabitants of certain territory therein defined. The provisions of this treaty are similar to the foregoing.

By treaty No. 5, made at Berens' River, 20th September, and at Norway House, on 24th September, 1875, the Saulteaux and Swampy Cree Tribes cede a certain tract of territory embracing an area of one hundred thousand square miles, more or less. The provisions are similar to those of the other treaties, with certain slight exceptions.

Treaty No. 6 was made on 23rd and 28th August, and on 9th September, 1876, respectively, with the Plain and Wood Cree Indians and other tribes at Fort Carleton, Fort Pitt, and Battle River. Reserves to the extent of one square mile for each family of five, or in that proportion, are set aside, and some of the other provisions are even more onerous to Canada than those of the foregoing treaties. The territory included in this treaty is approximately estimated to contain 120,000 square miles.

The Dominion has by these treaties acquired nearly the whole of the territory within the fertile belt, and for some distance North of it; in fact all the lands East of the Rocky Mountains with the exception of a small district of about 35,000 square miles inhabited by the Blackfeet Indians, about 4,000 souls. These Indians are anxious for a treaty to be made with them.* In regard to these Blackfeet, the departmental report says :—" It would appear that " the Blackfeet, who some twelve or fifteen years ago num- " bered upwards of ten thousand souls, and were then re- " markable as a warlike and haughty nation, have within " the last decade of years been greatly demoralized, and re- " duced by more than one-half their number—partly in " consequence of the poisoned fire-water introduced into " the territory by American traders, partly by the murder- " ous acts of lawless men from the American territory, and " partly by the terrible scourge of the Red man, small-pox, " which in 1870 caused great havoc among the Indians in " this region."

The Indians embraced under these six treaties number 17,754.

The expenditure in Manitoba and the North-West by the Dominion Government during the year ending 30th June, 1876, was $203,295 against $223,525 appropriated.

The Indians are gradually settling on the grounds allotted to them, and are commencing to understand the necessity of devoting themselves to agricultural pursuits, and in some instances considerable progress in this direction has already been made; the proximity of White settlements is

---

* A treaty with these Blackfeet has, we believe, been negotiated since the date of the departmental report now in our hands.

also of advantage, in that they can supply themselves on the same terms as other inhabitants of the Province with any articles they may require, and can also find a ready market for the products of the Hunt and of their Fishing.

In 1875 the Sioux Indians coming from the United States were, after due consideration, allowed reserves of 80 acres to every five persons, and tracts of country were according-ly surveyed at the mouth of Oak River comprising 7,936 acres, and at Bird Tail River near Fort Ellice comprising 6,885 acres, with which the Indians interested seemed to be well pleased, and at once started their gardens and commenced the construction of their dwellings.

Since this these Sioux have less frequently visited the settlements of the Western part of the Province, where their presence was always the subject of complaints, owing to their begging and thieving propensities, and it is consi-dered that once they get accustomed to living on their reserve, and cultivating the ground, all reason for complaint against them will have disappeared. In regard to these Indians Lieut.-Governor Morris in his report says:—" I " am sanguine that this settlement will prove a success, as " these Sioux are displaying a laudable industry in cutting " hay for their own use and for sale, and in breaking up " ground for cultivation."

Another addition of Sioux to the Indian population of that country has recently taken place, being those who have sought refuge there under Sitting Bull. In some quarters the Dominion was promised much trouble and annoyance from these Indians, but so far they have con-ducted themselves very peaceably and quietly, expressing their admiration for the British, their desire to settle down in the country, and their determination to obey the laws in every respect. Indeed it is wonderful what an ascendancy the officers of the Mounted Police have apparently obtain-ed over them, and it is noteworthy that if they profess implicit confidence in British impartiality, Major Walsh and his officers seem also to repose some considerable confidence in their protestations. It is true we have had a report within the past few days that Sitting Bull is endeavouring to stir up a feeling amongst the Blackfeet against the Whites in connection with the Buffalo Protection Act, but it is since said that this report has been started by the Half-breeds who are enraged at the Police for preventing them from exterminating the Buffalo. Sitting Bull and his band may yet give trouble, but no one in Canada doubts that if they should transgress the impartial laws under the protection of which they are now living, they would be sharply and effectually dealt with, even if it should require another Manitoban expedition under a second Colonel (now Sir Garnet) Wolseley to do it. And there is also reason to believe that in such an event the Indians of the North-West would, to a large extent, stand by the British and Canadian Governments, as it will be remembered that in 1875 the Blackfeet before alluded to were invited by the Sioux from the American side to join them in warring against the Whites, a proposition which they readily declined, and for so doing received the thanks of the Queen, who directed that they should be officially informed of her gratification at this evidence of their loyalty and attachment. However, it is more than likely that Sitting Bull's band, as well as any other band who may find themselves in that country, will appreciate too highly the laws in force, to lightly violate them.

The length of this paper forbids our noticing, otherwise than superficially, the British Columbia Indians. Suffice it to say they are described as a hardy, industrious race; those of the interior being extensive owners of stock, and having considerable agricultural knowledge, and those on the coast being expert fishermen, and many of them very comfortably off, though much given to gambling. Arrangements as to reserves will have to be made with them similar to those made in Manitoba.

We must not omit to state that missionaries are now also doing a good work among the Indians in the North-West and elsewhere, and rapidly extending their influence.

One or two extracts from reports may now be appended in closing :—

Lieut.-Governor Morris in his report says :—

" If the measures suggested by me are adopted, viz.,
" effective regulations with regard to the buffalo, the
" Indians taught to cultivate the soil, and the erratic half-
" breeds encouraged to settle down, I believe that the solu-
" tion of all social questions of any present importance in
" the North-West Territories will have been arrived at."

Speaking of the Mounted Police he says :—

" The conduct of the men was excellent, and the pre-
" sence of the force as an emblem and evidence of the
" establishment of authority in the North-West was of
" great value."

Commissioner Reid in his report says :—

" I would here mention that previous to my departure
" from Norway House there was a very hearty and appa-
" rently sincere expression of gratitude, on the part of all
" the Indians present, for the liberality extended to them,
" and a general and spoken wish that their thanks be con-
" veyed to the Queen's Representative in this Province for
" his kind interest in their welfare."

And Commissioner Dickieson says :—

" Besides the Sioux Chiefs, White Cap and Standing
" Buffalo, who have now lived on our territory for some
" years, I met at Qu'Appelle a delegation of Sioux from the
" United States.   *   *   *   They expressed the most
" perfect confidence in the British Government, and their
" desire always to be on good terms with those who lived
" on this side of the boundary line ; a state of things which
" has resulted from the manner in which their ancestors
" were treated, and the report of which has been handed
" down from father to son for several generations."

In conclusion, we see in the North West an immense
tract of country, peopled by savage and warlike races, with
as yet a small white population, and almost the only representatives of armed authority a handful of Mounted Police.
What is it that makes the native tribes so tractable and docile that life and property may now be considered safe ?
Is it the knowledge that behind the Mounted Police there
is force sufficient to crush out all disorder ? Is it the pres-
tige of British authority as represented by its army ? Partly
so no doubt, but not altogether. The reason is to be ascribed rather to equitable laws and generous treatment, and in
these respects the Canadian Government is raising up in
that vast country a monument to British authority that
shall endure for all time, a monument in which strict justice forms the base, kindness the shaft, and the whole
power of the British Empire the capital overlooking and
adorning the rest. These, and these alone are the secret
of the success of British authority in the North-West.